Patterns

Cynthia Rider

OXFORD
UNIVERSITY PRESS

This is a snowflake.

This lace mat is like a snowflake.

A spider can make patterns.

This climbing frame is like a spider's web.

A butterfly has patterns
on its wings.

This pattern is made of glass.
It looks like a butterfly wing.

honeycomb

Honey bees made this pattern.

A football looks like
a honeycomb.

Some patterns are hard to see.

Look for the snake. It looks like the ground.

Look for the truck. It looks like the ground.

The sea made this pattern
on the sand.

This paper has a
pattern like the sand.

13

The frost made this pattern.
It looks like leaves.

This pattern is made of stone.
It looks like leaves too.

Some children made
this pattern.